1. Soldiers of the élite *Sayeret Haruv* paratroop reconnaissance unit patrol the Suez Canal area, 1969. Their British paratroop helmets are covered with netting, held in place with strips of rubber tyre inner tubes. The two men in the front seat wear older British and American helmets. (IDF Archives)

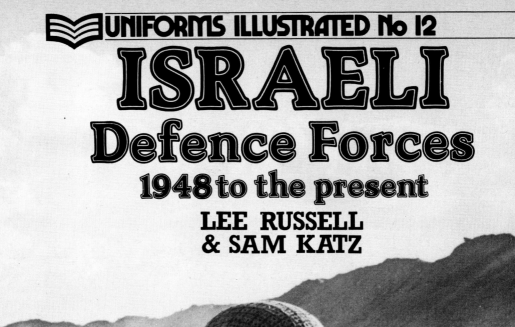

UNIFORMS ILLUSTRATED No 12

ISRAELI
Defence Forces
1948 to the present

LEE RUSSELL
& SAM KATZ

Introduction

...blished in 1985 by Arms and Armour Press,
.. Hampstead High Street, London NW3 1QQ.

..tributed in the United States by
..rling Publishing Co. Inc., 2 Park Avenue,
..w York, N.Y. 10016.

..blished in 1985 in Israel by
..imatzky's Agency Limited, Citrus House,
..B. 628, Tel-Aviv, Israel.

..itish Library Cataloguing in Publication Data:
..ssell, Lee
..aeli defence forces 1940 to the present. –
..niforms illustrated; v. 11)
..Israel. Tsera haganoch le-Yisrael – Uniforms
..listory
..Title   II. Katz, Sam   III. Series
..5.1'4'095694   UC485.18
..BN 0-85368-755-2

..iting, design and artwork by Roger Chesneau.
..pesetting by Typesetters (Birmingham) Ltd.
..nted in Italy by Tipolitografia G. Canale
..C. S.p.A., Turin, in association with Keats
..ropean Ltd.

The State of Israel was born a nation at war, and its first soldiers fought their battles in whatever they possessed – civilian clothes, odds and ends of British and American uniform and the occasional cartridge belt or steel helmet. The situation improved somewhat after the first few months, but standardization had to wait until the post-1949 period. For the first decade, the Israeli Defence Forces were clothed and equipped largely from British stockpiles abandoned in 1948. Nevertheless, by the early 1950s the IDF was producing its own combat uniforms, the style of which showed a strong American influence; by the late 1950s the IDF was also making some of its own web gear, although another decade would pass before it could completely replace the Second World War surplus in use.

The IDF's original types of combat clothing were not entirely satisfactory, and development continued throughout the 1960s. Meanwhile the Israelis acquired large stocks of French uniforms (especially 'lizard' pattern camouflage suits) made surplus by the end of the war in Algeria. These saw much use during the 1967 Arab–Israeli War but were phased out shortly thereafter, to be replaced by new IDF patterns, including olive fatigues and an excellent winter parka. Initial shortages were made up by issuing American items, including fatigues and field jackets, some of which remain in service with second-line units in 1985. The old stocks of British battle-dress, now relegated to Service Dress, finally gave out in the early 1970s and were replaced by a shirt-and-trousers 'A' Uniform.

In the late 1970s the Israelis also introduced a new pattern of load-bearing equipment, based on their own combat experience; like all Israeli military equipment, it was ingenious, practical and 'user-friendly'. At the same time, indigenous patterns of protective clothing, including helmets, flak vests and fire-resistant coveralls, came into service. Often these were based on equivalent American items which had served as a stop-gap, but they incorporated improvements in material technology. In addition to equipping the IDF, many of these items have been sold abroad, earning Israel much-needed foreign revenue.

The authors would like to thank the following for their assistance or the use of photographs: the IDF Spokesman, the Israeli Government Press Office (IGPO), the IDF Archives, the Israeli Air Force and Ministry of Defence, Andreas Constantinou and Reni Moza. Author Samuel M. Katz also wishes to thank his fellow IDF veteran Dan Rosenberg for his patience and technical assistance, and to offer a very special word of thanks to Sigalit Elyakim, without whose hard work, devotion and dedication this book would not have been possible.

Lee Russell and Sam Katz

.2
. One of the *Tzanchanim* (paratroopers) who
..mped at Mitla, October 1956. He is wearing the
..reen fatigues and a US steel helmet (modified by the
..DF with a new suspension). His parachute is French
..nd his two American pouches indicate that he is a
..nedic. He is armed with the Uzi SMG. (IGPO)

3. A squad of infantry scans the road to Jerusalem during the 1948 War of Independence. The men are wearing a mixture of British and American items, including British battle-dress and KD (khaki drill) uniforms, steel helmets, gaiters and puttees. The man on the extreme right has a US Army fatigue shirt. The webbing is a mixture of British and American patterns, and the men are armed with Sten guns and Czech Mauser rifles. (IDF Archives)

4. Israeli soldiers of the Southern Command pose by an Egyptian 2pdr gun captured in the Negev. Note the diverse combinations of ex-British, captured Egyptian and civilian clothing – for example, the man on the far left of the photograph is wearing a British sweater and battle-dress trousers, with a US cartridge belt and a US Navy telephone talker's helmet. Several men wear the IDF's first indigenous uniform item – a Canadian-looking field cap with integral neck flap. (IGPO)

5. During the battle for Jerusalem, 1948, a patrol set out through the rubble of the Old City. The newly issued *Tzahal* (the Hebrew acronym for *Tzeva Haganah le-Israel* – Israeli Defence Force) badge is worn on the field cap. The soldiers wear US cartridge belts and carry Czech Mauser rifles. The field cap was phased out in early 1950. (IGPO)

6. Machine-gunners near Kibbutz Yad Mordechai await an Egyptian attack, 1948. They are wearing civilian clothing and British steel helmets, and are armed with a Czech-supplied German MG34 light machine gun. (IGPO)

▲3   ▼4

▲7

7. Israeli soldiers pose after defeating an Egyptian force in the Faluja Pocket. They are wearing a great variety of uniforms and equipment, and are armed with Lee Enfields, PIATs, MG34s and Mauser rifles. (IGPO)

8. A *Sheulei Shimshon* (Samson's Foxes) raiding party of Southern Command, October 1948. Note the stretchers on the jeep. (IDF Archives)

9. A machine-gun post in Jerusalem, 1948. The soldier aiming the Besa machine gun is wearing a British KD shirt and shorts, with U web gear and grenade pouch. (IDF Archives)

▼8

9

10. Besa machine-gunners from an early mechanized brigade, near Ramla, 1948. The are wearing British 194 Pattern web gear, to which the nearer man has awkwardly fitted ar American field dressing pouch, canteen and Kabar knife. (IDF Archives)

11. A *Palmach* (pre-*Tzahal* Jewish under-ground army) sniper, now incorporated in the new Israeli Army, awai the enemy outside Jerusalem, 1948. He sti wears his *Palmach* patc on his uniform, and he armed with a British Lee-Enfield No. 4 rifle with sniper's scope. Around his head is a British camouflage veil, and a close combat knif is worn on his belt. (ID Archives)

12. Israeli soldiers in th Negev opposite Egyptian positions, 1949. Their uniforms and equipment are British, although the nearest man also has an American M1943 en-trenching tool. Berets began to be issued in 1949, and are worn here by two of the soldiers. (IDF Archives)

▲10   ▼11

12

▲13

▲14 ▼15

13. A group of ex-*Palmachnikim* in the Negev Desert, 1948. They are wearing British KD shirts and shorts, berets and field caps, British Mk. 1 steel helmets and even a British airborne helmet (probably obtained from a 6th Airborne Division soldier by one means or other). The IDF initially had to obtain its weaponry from any and every source: shown here are MG34s, Mausers, Lee-Enfields, Sten guns and even a Thompson SMG. (IDF Archives)

14. A sniper team near Jerusalem, 1948. The hills surrounding the city were the scene of much bitter fighting during the Arab Legion siege of the city. The sniper wears American HBT fatigues and a US cartridge belt, and a British camouflage veil covers his head; his assistant wears a British airborne helmet, sweater and web gear. (IDF Archives)

15. IDF trainees during a parade in 1950. They are wearing British battle-dress and American cartridge belts and carry Czech Mauser rifles. Following the War of Independence, the IDF took on a rather British appearance, owing mainly to the large volume of British uniforms left behind. Note the netting and foliage placed on the helmets. (IGPO)

16. Yesterday's cadets rejoice as today's officers in the emerging Israeli Navy (*Heyl Hayam*), 21 June 1955. In the years prior to 1962, anyone qualifying as officer material was accepted, even older veterans, as can be seen by the ages and 1948 campaign ribbons of some of the graduates. These officers are wearing the white dress uniform, old-style 'anchor' rank insignia and navy blue waist-belts; several men also wear the IDF Parachute badge. (IGPO)

17. IDF *Ramatkal* (Chief of Staff) Lt.Gen. Moshe Dayan boards an Israeli warship, November 1955. He is wearing British battle-dress, which was the IDF's main dress uniform until the mid-1970s. He also wears the brown rimmed IDF officer's peaked cap with the IDF General Staff badge; two smaller versions of this insignia are worn on the collar. Gen. Dayan also wears Israeli parachute wings and the 1948 campaign ribbon. The sailors are wearing the naval dress uniform for cool weather, with white leggings. The caps have 'Israeli Navy' written on the band in yellow Hebrew letters. The single stripe on one sailor's arm indicates the rank of *Tarash* (Lance-Corporal). (IGPO)

16▲   17▼

▲18　▼19

20 ▲

A morning inspection of an anti-aircraft unit in 1955. At this me the Armoured Corps was responsible for anti-aircraft duties, d all these personnel wore black berets. The figure in the centre is *Seren* (captain), as indicated by the three bars on his epaulettes; he also wearing the 1948 campaign ribbon and an early unit tag for e AA battalion. Note the 40mm Bofors gun in the background. (AF)

. Israeli tankers pose by a knocked-out Egyptian Sherman tank ring the 1956 Sinai campaign. They are wearing a wide sortment of uniforms, including Israeli-manufactured khaki-tan tigues, British battle-dress, Soviet bloc tanker's helmets and the wly issued tanker's black beret with Armoured Corps badge. though most of the men still carry Sten guns, the soldier on the treme right cradles the Israeli-made Uzi 9mm SMG first troduced in 1955. (IDF Archives)

. A squad of the paratroops who jumped into the strategic Mitla Pass in the Sinai, 29 October 1956. They wear Israeli-manufactured jump jackets and special ammunition pouches (note the man with the cigarette) to hold the 9mm magazines of the Uzi SMG. They still use British airborne helmets and their vehicle is armed with an MG34 left over from the 1948 war. The officer at far left is Maj. Rafael 'Raful' Eitan, who would later become Israel's eleventh Chief of Staff, holding this office during the 1982 war in the Lebanon. (IDF Archives)

21. Israeli military police officers being interviewed in Gaza, November 1956. The officer with the wooden-stocked Uzi is wearing the officer's peaked cap with *Mishtera Tzvai* (Military Police) cap badge. The device on his collar is the *Sikat Memmem*, indicating graduation from the officer's course. He also wears a 1948 campaign ribbon. Slip-on rank insignia are worn on the epaulettes and a red/blue MP arm band on the right arm. (IDF Archives)

21 ▼

22. An Israeli paratrooper examines a captured Egyptian SKS rifle in Sinai, 1956. He is wearing a French airborne camouflage jacket – uncharacteristic, but not unheard-of. H[e] also wears Israeli-made olive green fatigue trousers and brown paratroop boots. Note the Infantry badge on his red paratroop beret. (IDF Archives)

23. An Israeli major (with ber[et] and goggles) and a first lieutenant examine a captured RPD machine gun. They both wear khaki tan fatigues, and t[he] lieutenant's jacket is made fro[m] a cut-down army sweater. His rank insignia consist of two bronze metal bars on his epaulettes, whilst the major prefers the cloth slip-on type. (IDF Archives)

24. *Golani* infantry during a training exercise. An élite infantry unit, the *Golani* Brigade specializes in mounta[in] warfare and is known for its physical toughness and skill a[t] fieldcrafts. The soldiers are armed with the Galilon SAR (Short Assault Rifle) version o[f] the 5.56mm Galil assault rifle. (IDF Spokesman)

25. An M113 crew in the Lebanon, wearing the new Type 602 CVC (Combat Vehi[cle] Crewman) helmets and flak jackets, 1983. (IDF Spokesman)

▲22   ▼23

26. A female paratrooper corporal in the new (1982) female 'A' Uniform, with red airborne headgear. The red backing to her Infantry beret badge and campaign ribbon indicate that she was a soldier during the Lebanon War. (Samuel M. Katz)

27. Paratroops from the *Sayeret Matkal* (the reconnaisance commando unit of the General Staff) in the Jebel Barouk mountains of Lebanon's Beka'a Valley, January 1983. Their white camouflage overgarments and *Hermoniot* snow boots (very similar to Second World War US shoepacs and developed from the same Canadian design) were specially developed for the snowy Lebanese winters. Regular web gear is worn, with extra equipment carried in white camouflaged rucksacks. Note the mountain pick carried by the figure in the centre, who is armed with a CAR-15 SAR. (IDF Spokesman)

28. The first Israelis to reach the Suez Canal in 1956; the fatigue of the 100-hour dash across Sinai can clearly be seen. All the men are armed with the Czech Mauser and are wearing Israeli khaki-tan fatigues with British helmets and webbing and carry US canteens and entrenching tools. Note also the bayonet for the *Czechi* (as the Israelis called the Mauser) and the fact that the man on the left with the rocket launcher still wears his old-type field hat under his helmet. (IDF Archives)

29. A souvenir from Operation 'Kadesh' – a picture of Egyptian leader Gamal Nasser. The soldier's khaki-tan fatigue shirt bears the *Tzahal* stencil above the right pocket. (IDF Archives)

▲26 ▼27

▲30   ▼31

30. A squad of Israeli infantrymen mans a position in Sinai, 1956. All wear the khaki-tan fatigues and are armed with a mixed assortment of weapons – a Sten gun, a Mauser and an early Uzi. The automatic weapon is a Belgian FN Type D light machine gun. Note the officer's gaiters, phased out after the 1956 war, and the khaki-brown Infantry beret on the ground beside the British 1937 Pattern small pack. (IDF Archives)

31. Another view of one of the *Tzanchanim* who jumped at the Mitla Pass. He is wearing the belted green jump jacket, British 1937 Pattern web gear and modified US steel helmet, and his parachutes are packed in a kitbag on his back. (IGPO)

32. Israeli Mystère IVA pilots prepare for an operational mission in November 1956. They are wearing American G-4B coveralls with built-in g-suit, the American P-4B helmet with A-13 oxygen mask, and the B-5 life preserver, with *Tzahal* stencil. Note the pistol holster and survival knife strapped to the right leg of the man on the left. (IDF Archives)

33. A group of Israeli soldiers relaxing near a UN position in the Sinai, 1957. They are wearing their olive drab 'A' Uniforms and red paratroop berets. The brass Infantry badge with its red plastic background (indicating combat service) can clearly be seen. (United Nations)

34. A photograph of an Israeli sailor taken about 1957. His white and navy blue cap has the Naval badge in gold-coloured brass and his ship's name, INS *Misgav*, printed in yellow. This style of cap was later phased out, to be replaced by a navy blue beret with a larger Naval badge in gold, and the uniform has been replaced by khaki or white fatigues similar to those worn by the Army. (IGPO)

35. A group of Israeli Border Guards assembles in the New City of Jerusalem, just prior to the outbreak of the June 1967 Six-Day War. They are wearing the Israeli khaki-tan 'A' Uniform with black combat boots. The web gear is the pattern adopted by the Israeli Defence Forces from 1956, and is based on a combination of American and British patterns, and the pouches were specially designed to hold the magazines of the FN FAL rifle, which became the mainstay of the IDF in the late 1950s. The pistol belt was adaptable to such additions as the special Uzi pouches and extra canteens. The Border Guards are part of the Israeli National Police, not the Army, and are responsible for security within Israel's borders, ports of entry and occupied areas. They use a rank system different from that of the IDF, and still retain the British-style chevrons; their beret is dark green with the National Police badge. The man with his back to the camera seems to have obtained a US Marine jungle first aid pouch and is carrying an American M1 carbine. (IDF Archives)

▲ 34   ▼ 35

36▲   37▼

36. In the late 1950s the Israelis obtained large quantities of French 'lizard' pattern camouflage uniforms for their troops; one of these is worn by this soldier guarding Egyptian prisoners of war in Rafah, June 1967. He is armed with the Belgian FN FAL rifle, produced under licence in Israel and modified to IDF specifications, and is wearing British 1944 pattern belt and braces (the latter modified to accept a US M1943 entrenching tool) and equipped with the new plastic IDF canteen and frog for FN bayonet. The French bush hat was worn in large numbers by the Israelis during the 1967 war. (IGPO)

37. The IAF commander at the time of the Six-Day War, Maj.Gen. Mordechai Hod, in the khaki 'A' uniform worn at the time by IAF personnel. His officer's peaked cap is greyish-blue with a black brim and IAF cap badge; the backing for his rank insignia is also greyish-blue, with silver devices, and the ribbons are for the 1948 and 1956 campaigns. This photograph provides an excellent view of the Israeli pilot's wings insignia. (IGPO)

▲ 38

▼ 39

38. Israeli paratroopers prepare for the jump into
Sinai that never came, 6 June 1967. They are wearing
British paratroop helmets, indigenous web gear and
brown paratroop boots, with French parachutes. The
transport is a French Nord Noratlas. (IGPO)

39. Col. 'Raful' Eitan (with cap) in Rafah, during the
Israeli advance into Sinai. He is wearing an Israeli
field jacket with IDF web gear, including the Uzi
magazine pouch. As a brigade commander, he is
wearing goggles for his command vehicle over his
issue field cap. The insignia on his sleeve is that of the
202nd Airborne Brigade; usually worn as a removable
'tag', it is here sewn to the sleeve. The other officer is
equipped with the IDF canteen and carrier and the
magazine pouch for the FN rifle. Their tired and
bearded faces show the effects of the hard-fought
battle for Rafah. (IGPO)

40. The command post of Col. Mordechai Gur,
whose paratroops captured the Old City of Jerusalem
in the Six-Day War, to reunite it with the rest of the
Israeli capital. His men are wearing a mixture of
'lizard' camouflage, olive and khaki-tan fatigue
uniforms, British paratroop helmets and IDF web
gear. The radiomen carry Israeli-made Mk.25 radios
(licence-produced copies of the US AN/PRC-25)
attached to US packboards. Note also the man with
map case. (IGPO)

41. Israeli sailors on board a patrol boat cruising in
the Straits of Tiran, off the coast of Sinai. They are
wearing British Mk.1 steel helmets, life jackets and
the 1950s-type olive fatigue trousers with one pocket
on each leg. (IGPO)

▲ 42

42. A bazooka team operating in the Old City of Jerusalem against the Jordanian Arab Legion. They wear the old-style olive fatigues (note the single rear pocket on the right side only) with British 1944 Pattern web gear and steel helmets. Their first lieutenant wears the khaki-tan fatigue shirt. (IGPO)

43. Chief of Staff Lt.Gen. Yitzach Rabin conferring with Defence Minister Moshe Dayan during the campaign in Sinai, June 1967; he is wearing the officer's peaked cap with General Staff cap badge and unit tag, the insignia symbolizing the combined services of the Army, Air Force and Navy. His decorations include paratroop wings and campaign ribbons for the 1948 and 1956 wars. (IDF Archives)

44. Israeli Border Guards stand watch outside the Wailing Wall in Jerusalem following its capture by Israeli forces. The beret badge can be clearly seen, as well as the tan 'A' Uniform and Israeli FAL. (IDF Archives)

▼ 43

▼ 44

45. Infantry advance through the Syrian-held Golan Heights, 8 June 1967, dressed in a mix of French 'lizard'-camouflage and khaki-tan uniforms and armed with Uzis, FN rifles and a Belgian bazooka. The assistant bazooka gunner carries extra rockets on a US packboard. (IDF Archives)

46. Paratroop radiomen and their officer during the battle for the Police School in Jerusalem, 1967, offer a good view of the IDF canteen and the modified suspension of the British paratroop helmet. The man on the left wears the old-type khaki-tan fatigues; both radiomen use US Army packboards to carry their Mk.25 radios, and one man has found a field-expedient method of holding the handset, tucking it under his helmet straps! Note also the folding-stock Uzis. (IDF Archives)

46 ▼

▲47   ▼48

47. A paratroop rifleman covers his companions during the advance through the Old City of Jerusalem. He is dressed in the 1950s-type green fatigues with IDF-type web gear. (IDF Archives)

48. A conference of division commanders and their subordinates in the Sinai. The Israeli generals, Maj.Gen. Yisrael Tal and Yehoshoua Gavish (with beret and goggles at far right), both wear the green fatigues, whilst the soldier with the French bush hat wears the khaki-tan type. Note the slip-on rank insignia and black berets (with Artillery badge) of the Artillery colonels (*Aluf Mishne*), and also the Air Force liaison officer wearing the peaked cap and sunglasses at rear. The high degree of informality that has existed in the IDF since its inception is evident here. (IDF Archives)

49. An Israeli reservist on the Jerusalem front. He is wearing khaki-tan fatigues, an unmodified US steel helmet and British 1944 Pattern web gear, with a 1937 small pack and IDF canteen. He is armed with a Czech Mauser. (IGPO)

50. Israeli *Chayalot* (female soldiers) undergo training in late 1967. They are wearing the female version of the khaki fatigue uniform with brown khaki sweater. The corporal instructor is wearing a green lanyard, indicating her status as an instructor. (IGPO)

49 ▲   50 ▼

29

▲51 ▼52

▲53 ▼54

51. Israeli Women's Corps (*Chen*) 'A' Uniform, about 1968. All women soldiers wear black headgear, except for those assigned to Paratroop units (who wear red), the *Golani* Infantry Brigade (brown) and the Air Force (blue-grey). Foot wear is left to the discretion of the individual, but must be black in colour; most women soldiers wear sandals. (IDF Spokesman)

52. An Israeli Air Force officer in 'A' Uniform, 1968 – blue-grey RAF battle-dress, worn with a white shirt. (IDF spokesman)

53. A paratrooper in 'A' Uniform of olive belted jacket and trousers, red beret and brown paratroop boots, about 1968. Jump wings are worn above the left breast pocket. (IDF Spokesman)

54. An Israeli *Golani* Infantryman, 1968, in field uniform of French 'lizard' camouflage, French bush hat and black combat boots. (IDF Spokesman)

55. A female member of a paratroop brigade, 1968. She wears her Parachute Rigger's badge beneath her blue-backed jump wings and has Corporal's stripe sewn on both sleeves. (IDF Spokesman)

56. An Israeli recon paratrooper, 1968. He is a member of the *Sayeret Shaked*, until 1983 the Airborne Reconnaisance Unit of the Southern Command, equivalent to the US Army's LRRPs or Marine Force Recon units. He wears the current IDF olive fatigues with black beret and red-backed Infantry badge (indicating combat service); beneath his jump wings he wears the special *Sayeret* (Reconnaisance) wings, awarded on completion of a difficult eleven-month course. He is also a veteran of the 1967 war, as shown by his campaign ribbon. The three stripes pinned to his left sleeve indicate the rank of *Samal*, or Sergeant. (IDF Spokesman)

57. In 1968 units of the IDF crossed the border into Jordan in an operation to destroy Palestinian terrorist bases near the town of Karameh; these paratroops are attacking a PLO position there. The white stripes attached to the helmet are for station-keeping on night patrol. The man in the centre, cocking his Uzi, wears two pouches next to his canteen for holding grenades. Two men carry FN rifles, one fitted with a bipod and one with anti-tank grenades, very useful for fighting in built-up areas. (IDF Archives)

55▲   56▲   57▼

▲58 ▼59

32

58. An Israeli Border Guard stands sentry on the Lebanese border, January 1970. His web gear is worn over his IDF-issue winter parka, and his headgear is the winter cap, still in use. Note the number of rifle grenades situated to the left of the position! (IGPO)
59. Maj.-Gen. Tal and Col. Shmuel Gonen talk with soldiers of the 7th Armoured Brigade at a base in the Golan, 1970. Col. Gonen (with glasses) wears the 7th Brigade's unit tag (*Taag Yechida*) as well as his black tanker's beret tucked under one epaulette. Brass officer's insignia is now worn only with the 'A' Uniform. (IDF Spokesman)
60. Military Police at the trial of a Palestinian terrorist in the early 1970s. They wear British battle-dress with khaki-tan shirts. The white-painted US helmet liners have the Hebrew letters *Mem* and *Tzadeh*, standing for *Mishtera Tzvai*, painted in red. Note the manner in which the soldier on the left carries the extra magazine for his Uzi tucked into the weapon's sling. (IDF Spokesman)
61. In a 1970 operation Israeli paratroopers captured Shedwan Island in the Suez Canal from the Egyptians and held it long enough to fly out the latest Soviet air defence radars on the island. Note that the man on the extreme left is armed with an AK-47, by then an issue weapon for commando units of the IDF. (IDF Spokesman)

62. Israeli naval commandos in training, 1970. They wear standard commercial neoprene rubber wet-suits, double-hose regulators, yellow twin oxygen tanks and red buoyancy jackets. They are armed with Uzis and operate from a Zodiac rubber assault boat. (IGPO)

63. A 1982 photograph of an Israeli Missile Boat commander. He is wearing the standard IDF olive fatigues, with blue and yellow rank insignia. Note the SAAR-3 missile boat in background. *Heyl Hayam)*

64. *Golani* infantry in the Lebanon, winter 1983. The officer speaking on the radio is wearing the Israeli winter parka, and the white tape on the rear of the helmet is for station-keeping on night marches. The radioman carries the Israeli-made Mk.25 radio and Galil rifle, whilst the officer has the Galilon SAR. (IDF Spokesman)

 62

63▲ 64▼

▲ 65 ▼ 66

65. *Ramatkal* (Chief of Staff) Lt.Gen. Moshe Levy chats with troops during exercises in the Jordan Valley, 1984. Originally from an Airborne unit, he still possesses his red beret (under the epaulette) and brown paratroop boots. (IDF Spokesman)

66. A female soldier of the Israeli Air Force, in the older female 'A' Uniform, with blue-grey Air Force cap with IAF beret badge and unit tag. (*Heyl Havir*)

67. Another group of Israeli paratroopers on Shedwan Island. They are wearing a prototype of the load-bearing blouse that became standard in the late 1970s and a mix of American OG 107 and Israeli fatigue uniforms. The soldier second from the right is a medic (note his medical pouches) and is armed with an AK-47 assault rifle, whilst the soldier in the centre has wrapped the bipod of his FN FAL with cloth to make a more comfortable hand-grip. (IGPO)

68. Air Force Day 1972: pilots receive their wings following a two-year training course. Guests of honour include Defence Minister Dayan and Chief of Staff Lt.Gen. Chaim Bar-Lev. Bar-Lev is wearing the khaki dress uniform phased out later that year. Note, far right, the Air Force lieutenant-colonel with a blue lanyard, indicating instructor status. (IDF Spokesman)

67▲ 68▼

▲69   ▼70

38

71 Chief of Staff Bar-Lev (right) and Col. Rafful Eitan, who would eventually hold the Chief of Staff post himself. Bar-Lev wears the olive 'B' Uniform with campaign ribbons for three wars, and parachute and pilot's wings (this version is for pilots who have received their training outside the IAF programme). Bar-Lev's black beret (he came from an armoured unit) is worn with General Staff badge and matching unit tag. Eitan also wears pilot's wings and Master Paratrooper wings, indicating over fifty jumps; they are backed in red, for his combat jump at the Mitla Pass. All other paratroops wear blue (qualification), white (instructor) or green (reconnaisance) backings to their wings. (IDF Spokesman)

72 Chief of Staff Bar-Lev inspecting naval units at Haifa, 1969. By this time the Navy was wearing khaki-tan 'A' uniforms, with white belts, but retained the white belts and leggings for ceremonial duties. Note the Israeli position of attention when armed with the Uzi SMG. (IDF Spokesman)

73 Chief of Staff Bar-Lev inspecting a tank unit in 1971. He is wearing the cool-weather 'A' uniform which was patterned after the British battle-dress of the IDF's early years. The tankers wear the Israeli Type I tanker's helmet, a licence-produced copy of the US CVC (Combat Vehicle Crewman) helmet; they also wear Nomex fire-resistant overalls and the standard Israeli pistol belt. (IDF Spokesman)

74 A view of the Nomex overalls from the rear. The white triangle on the helmets indicates the fire. (IDF Spokesman)

71▲   72▼

39

73. A military policeman brings in a Palestinian terrorist. He wears an American M65 field jacket and the peaked cap issued only to MPs. (IDF Spokesman)

74. A patrol of Israeli paratroops in Sinai during the War of Attrition with Egypt, 1970. They are wearing olive fatigues, a combination of French and American helmets, and standard webbing. (IDF Archives)

75. A mechanized patrol from the *Sayeret Shaked*, Sinai, 1970, with a mix of American and British airborne helmets. Netting is secured with strips of rubber inner tube. The vehicle's armament is a Belgian FN MAG GPMG. (IDF Archives)

76. *Golani* infantrymen undergoing live fire exercises in northern Israel prior to the outbreak of the 1973 war. The instructor wears the twin ammunition pouches for the Uzi SMG (which are joined at the back to form a single unit) and the two canteens carried by all Israeli soldiers. Both men wear Israeli-modified US M1 helmets and the current pattern IDF fatigues, and note the extra leg pocket of the instructor's uniform (this appears only on the left leg and is used to carry cigarettes or perhaps the soldier's wallet). The MAG gunner wears one of the several patterns of dust goggles used by the IDF. (IDF Archives)

▲73 ▼74

▲77

▲78

77. *Golani* infantrymen during a cross-border raid into Fatahland, Southern Lebanon, 1972, searching for PLO guerrillas. The 1937 knapsack (now produced in Israel under its original designation) indicates that the wearer is carrying extra grenades for his unit. In IDF infantry formations every man has a task other than that of rifleman – he might also carry anti-tank grenades, a radio, etc. – which makes the units more independent and increases their combat effectiveness. (IDF Spokesman)

78. A *Segen Mishne* (second lieutenant) of the élite 7th Armoured Brigade in 1973. His black tanker's beret is worn with a red-backed Armoured Corps badge, indicating combat service. (IDF Archives)

79. *Golani* infantrymen during another raid into Lebanon. Local terrain conditions make the use of the long-range radio antenna more necessary than, say, by US troops in Vietnam, who used the same radio. Note the strobe light carried by man in the centre. The tense atmosphere of such raids is reflected in the expression of the officer signalling to his men. (IDF Archives)

80. The same *Golani* unit, seen later during the same raid. The officer (a first lieutenant) is wearing a mask over his face to keep out dust, and he carries a flashlight for searching PLO tunnels. Magazines for his AK-47 are carried in a PLO or Syrian chest pouch, slung over one shoulder. (IDF Archives)

▼79

▼80

81▲

81. *Yom Kippur*, the Jewish Day of Atonement, is the holiest of all Jewish holidays. In 1973 it fell on 6 October, and at 2 p.m. on that day the Syrian Army crossed the Golan Heights and attacked Israeli positions; at the same moment, in a co-ordinated attack, the Egyptians crossed the Suez Canal and pushed into Israeli-held Sinai. The war was hard-fought and brutal on occasion. Here, men from a 155mm SP howitzer battery relax during a break in the fighting. Except for one man with a parka, all wear flak jackets, mostly US M1952 pattern but including (man at left) the indigenous Israeli type. Exhaustion is evident on every face. (IDF Archives)

82. Three soldiers from *Sayeret Golani*, the recon unit of the *Golani* Brigade, after recapturing the strategic Mount Hermon position from the Syrians, 23 October 1973. Their uniforms are a mixture of olive IDF and US OG 107 fatigues. (IDF Archives)

82 ▼

▲ 83 ▼ 84

85 ▲

◄86

83. A Centurion tank commander on the Golan Heights during the 1973 war, wearing the Nomex coveralls and Type 601 helmet. Although obsolete in American service, this helmet is still used by the IDF in 1985. (IDF Archives)

84. IDF combat engineers advance into Syria during the 1973 war. The standing soldier wears an older type winter jacket – a garment which was not particularly warm and one which was unpopular with the troops. (IDF Archives)

85. 7th Armoured Brigade commander Lt.Col. Avigdor Kahalani (right) and one of his officers, just after the battle in the 'Valley of Tears', where the Israelis stopped the Syrian advance in tank battles fought, at times, at a range of five yards. Kahalani, Israel's most brilliant tank commander, wears Nomex coveralls and the IDF pistol belt with holster and spare ammunition pouch. (IDF Archives)

86. A *Golani* infantryman takes a break from the fighting. He is wearing an American M1952 flak jacket, M1 steel helmet, and goggles. (IDF Archives)

45

87. A command post at Refidim in the Sinai, 14 October 1973. Note the introduction of the yellow *Tzahal* name-tape to the fatigue shirt. Girls work as communications officers and intelligence analysts, freeing the maximum number of men to serve in combat duties. (IDF Archives)

88. IDF soldiers catch up on news from the home front at an observation post by the Suez Canal, where they had surrounded and trapped the Egyptian Third Army. The casual appearance of the soldiers is typical of the IDF in war and peace. Note the Uzi with its two-clip attachment, a most interesting and useful device. (IDF Archives)

89. Soldiers from the *Sayeret Egoz* prepare to attack Egyptian positions on the west bank of the Suez Canal, 20 October 1973. The man with the rifle grenades carries the special grenade-launching cartridges in machine-gun links attached to his belt; the man with the RPG (then issued only to élite commando units but now a standard IDF infantry weapon) is also armed with an Uzi, the pouches for which he wears on his belt. The RPG rockets are carried in the issue RPG rocket bag. Note also the man with the Heavy-Barrel FAL and its padded bipod legs at the rear. (IDF Archives)

90. The attack coming on a Jewish Holy Day sparked religious fervour among some of the Orthodox soldiers, for example this man with phylacteries, prayer shawl and wooden-stocked Uzi. (IDF Archives)

▲87   ▼88

89 ▲   90 ▼

▲91   ▼92

91. A group of Israeli reservists in the ruins of Suez City, 1 December 1973. They are wearing American M65 field jackets and American and IDF fatigues. (United Nations/T.Nagata)
92. The crew of a missile boat during the 1973 October War, wearing standard fatigues, blue waist-belts, US steel helmets and French belt-type life preservers. (IGPO)
93. Military Police at a UN-supervised exchange of bodies, December 1973. They wear the olive 'A' Uniform, with white waist-belts, lanyards and helmets. (IGPO)
94. Maj.Gen. (Res.) Ariel 'Arik' Sharon at an Army press conference on the west bank of the Suez Canal, on the road to Ismailia. The tank officer beside him wears an unusual combination of metal and slip-on rank insignia. (IDF Archives)

93▲

94 ▼

▲95   ▼96

95. A wounded Egyptian prisoner of war being escorted to a Red Cross aircraft, with Israeli MPs supervising, November 1973. A wide variety of clothing can be seen, ranging from US field jackets and fatigues to the Israeli winter parka. Women soldiers wear the female spring jacket, used until the late 1970s, and black headgear piped in red, indicating their Military Police branch. (United Nations/Y.Nagata)

96. An Israeli armoured unit prepares to withdraw from Syrian territory, 18 June 1974. The men in the background are from the Israeli military band. Note the adjustment buckle to the IDF web belt on the soldier at right. (United Nations/Y.Nagata)

97. A woman instructor at the IDF Armoured Warfare School disembarks from an M60 tank. She wears a US Army aviator's two-piece Nomex flight suit and civilian shoes and carries the Type 601 helmet. The green Instructor's lanyard and Armoured Corps pin on her shirt indicate that this young woman is a qualified armoured crew member. (GPO)

98. MPs argue with women soldiers about military appearance, somewhere in Israel, 1975. Note that the IDF-pattern battle-dress 'A' Uniform is still being worn, as well as white sleeve covers for traffic control. The patch above the rank insignia is a Profession tag, indicating the course the soldier has passed; the stripes below the symbol show his degree of skill. Women soldiers wear either the female spring jacket or (centre) an obsolete pattern Air Force flight jacket. (GPO)

97▲   98▼

99. Following a PLO attack in Israel in March 1978 which killed 33 Israeli civilians, the IDF carried out a major incursion into southern Lebanon called Operation 'Litani'. Here a paratrooper patrols with his FN MAG. He is wearing standard olive fatigues with the new load-bearing blouse adopted in early 1978; the latter offered greater comfort and practicality in carrying equipment. Note the bag attached to the MAG to collect spent shells – even in combat, the thrifty IDF takes care to collect its spent brass for reloading! (IGPO)

100. *Golani* in southern Lebanon, March 1978. They wear the new load-bearing equipment with US flak jacket. The pouches can hold up to twelve M16, Galil or AK-47 magazines, two canteens and grenades. The soldier on the right has the tan rubber band for his helmet netting, an issue item by 1978. (United Nations/ J. K. Isaac)

101. Israeli soldiers prepare their withdrawal from southern Lebanon, to be replaced by UNIFIL troops, 30 March 1978. They wear US flak jacket and carry the Galil 5.56mm assault rifle issued to many front-line troops in 1978. (United Nations/J. K. Isaac)

▲ 99   ▼ 100   101▶

▲102   ▼103

102. Israeli sailors line up for inspection in 1978, wearing the white Naval 'A' Uniform, with navy blue waist-belts and black combat boots; later that year the navy blue beret with gold badge would be replaced by the white 'Popeye' hat. Rank insignia is a blue and gold version of the Army insignia – the IDF does not have a separate system for the Navy. (IDF Spokesman)

103. *Tat Aluf* (Brig.Gen.) Michael 'Yomi' Barakai, before a 1975 ceremony that would appoint him overall Navy commander and award him the rank of Major General. He is wearing the old-style white naval officer's peaked cap (the new style has a gold band below an enlarged Naval badge), with white dress uniform. His rank insignia is blue with gold devices. Over his left breast pocket is the Veteran Submariner's badge with red (combat) backing, the blue *Ot Hamophet* medal for bravery (there are three Israeli awards for heroism, but the standards for earning them are so high that few are actually awarded) and campaign ribbons for the 1956, 1967 and 1973 wars. On the pocket is a miniature version of the Missile Boat badge, and over his right pocket are blue-backed parachute wings. (IDF Spokesman)

104. A female *Rasal* (Master Sergeant) in the khaki-tan female 'A' Uniform, with olive green waist-belt and black headgear with *Heyl Shalishut* (Administrative Services) badge. Her unit tag is worn on her left arm and her profession patch on the right; she also wears the campaign ribbon of the 1973 war and the Operational Service badge. Rank insignia is worn as a wrist-band, with the brass Master Sergeant's device backed in red. (IDF Spokesman)

105. A *Golani* infantryman wearing IDF winter parka and US OG 107 fatigues. His brown beret is tucked under one epaulette. Note the *Golani* unit tag worn at the shoulder. (IDF Spokesman)

106. Combat engineers at a Negev training base in 1978, with a mixture of M16s and Galils. The two men on the left wear US-pattern fatigues, the other two the IDF type with *Tzahal* name-tape. Note the pinning of the corporal's tank insignia to the sleeve, a common IDF practice. (IDF Spokesman)

54

104▲ 105▲ 106▼

▲107 ▼108

109 ▲

107. On the rifle range with the Galil. Note the field cap and a rear view of the new web gear. (IDF Spokesman)

108. Combat engineers on an assault course, showing the assault slings of their rifles, including the American M16s. Although the Israelis have been issuing these slings for years, the US armed forces have yet to develop an equivalent item, and American troops must make do with every sort of field expedient instead. (IDF Spokesman)

109. An IAF Boeing 707 crew with Prime Minister Menachem Begin on a 1979 state visit to the United States. They wear the Israeli-made battle-dress style uniform with peaked caps and, in one case, the IAF blue beret. (IGPO)

▲110

110. Israeli naval commandos watch a work detail aboard INS *Aliyah*, a helicopter-carrying missile boat, June 1980. The commandos wear the summer black rubber wet-suit, and the sailors in the distance now wear the white 'Popeye' hat. (IGPO)

111. Newly appointed *Ramatkal* Lt.Gen. 'Raful' Eitan (centre) on a tour of an IDF Ordnance Corps base. In the rear are captured T-55 tanks in the process of being rebuilt as Israeli *Tirans*. General Eitan wears the red paratroop beret (he was formerly an Airborne officer) with General Staff badge, and along with his Master Paratroop

wings and campaign ribbons he wears the red *Ot Haoz* medal for bravery, earned on a cross-border raid in 1955. The small menorah clasp on his 1948 campaign ribbon indicates that he fought in the battle for Jerusalem. (IDF Spokesman)

112. Israeli paratroopers in training in the Jordan Valley, 1981, armed with CAR-15 and M16 rifles. The American weapons were first introduced after the 1973 War as a stop-gap until the Galil was in full production. (IGPO)

111▲ 112▼

▲113 ▼114

115▲

◀116

113. More paratroops undergoing training in the Jordan Valley in 1981. Note the introduction of the short-barrelled Galilon rifle carried by the officer on the right and the tape-covered ID disc of the soldier on the left. (IGPO)

114. Assistant Chief of Staff (now, in 1985, the current Chief of Staff) Maj.Gen. Moshe Levi observes training exercises in the Jordan Valley, March 1981. In place of the IDF-issue paratroop boots he wears a US Marine pair from the 1950s, with the IDF's grey socks. (IGPO)

115. A 20mm Oerlikon AA gunner aboard an Israeli missile boat, 1981. He is wearing standard fatigues, a West German life preserver and the Orlite infantry ballistic helmet. (IGPO)

116. On 6 June 1982, responding to PLO attacks on towns in the north of the country, Israel launched its invasion of Lebanon, Operation 'Peace for Gaililee'. Here paratroops armed with M16s carefully check an alley in the PLO stronghold of Tyre. Note the pointman's flashlight and US packboard, used to carry a folded stretcher. (IGPO)

▲117

117. IDF paratroops advance near the town of Sidon. They are wearing the new Israeli-made kevlar flak jacket and webbing and are armed with Galilon rifles and an FN MAG GPMG. Note the entrenching tool on the 1937 field pack carried by the soldier with the MAG and the stretcher carried on a US packboard. Helmet camouflage is individually applied, using shoe polish. (IMoD)

118. An M113 crew photographed on the coastal highway near Beirut. They are wearing the newly issued Type 602 tanker's helmet

▼118

and American M69 flak jackets. (IDF Spokesman)

119. Paratroops patrol the lines in the Beka'a Valley opposite Syrian positions in Lebanon. They carry LAW rockets and anti-tank grenades and wear the knee-pads issued for the Lebanon campaign. (IMoD)

120. Paratroopers about to be airlifted by helicopter to the fighting at the Ein Hilweh camp near Sidon. Note the issue kitbags and the Dragon anti-tank weapons. (IDF Spokesman)

▲121   ▼122   ▼123

124 ▲

121. An Israeli *Golani* infantryman with his issue RPG in Damour, June 1982. The issue tan rubber band holds his helmet netting in place, and extra plastic-covered rockets are stowed in the issue RPG bag. (IGPO)
122. IDF soldiers scale a wall during house-to-house searches near Sidon, 22 June 1982. (IGPO)
123. A *Nahal* paratrooper seen during the fighting for Beirut International Airport, August 1982. His Galil lacks a bipod but is fitted with a bayonet stud, and he carries a knapsack filled with rifle grenades. (IDF Spokesman)
124. An IDF position above the Bourj el Barajneh terrorist stronghold in West Beirut, 3 August 1982. The troops wear the new kevlar flak jackets but have removed their webbing, and they are armed with Galilon and MAG infantry weapons. (IGPO)
125. Paratroopers outside Beirut, 1982. Note the shaven heads, the Galilons, and the watch cover of the soldier on the right. (IGPO)

125 ▼

126. IDF soldiers guard the approaches to Deir Banoun, 7 June 1982. The pouch at the rear of the nearer soldier holds either medical equipment or extra ammunition. (IGPO)

127. Recon paratroops from the *Sayeret Shaked* during the battle for Ein Hilweh, June 1982. The pointman is armed with an AK-47. (IDF Spokesman)

128. An Israeli 155mm SP gun commander near Beirut, August 1982, wearing a US M69 flak jacket and the IDF-modified M1 steel helmet. (IGPO)

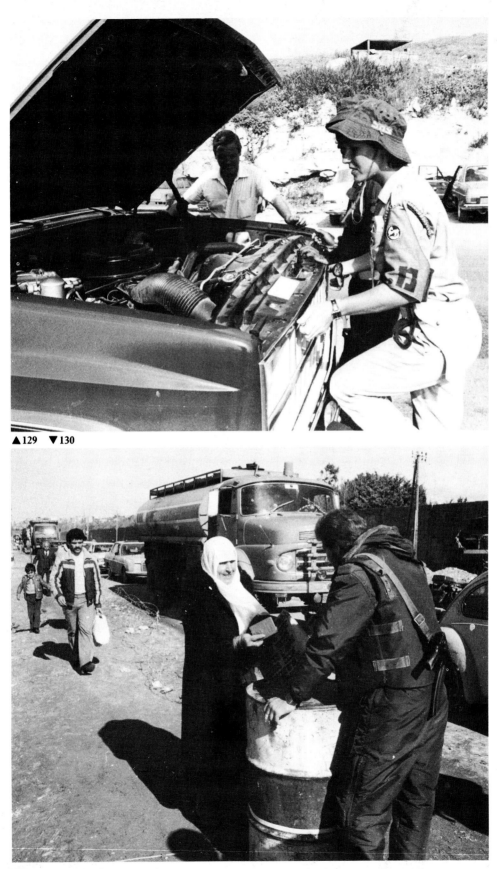

129. A female MP *Rasa* (Master Sergeant) checking Lebanese cars inside southern Lebanon, September 1982. She is wearing the khaki-tan service uniform, which was at that time in the process of being phased out in favour of olive fatigues like those of male soldiers. Her MP brassard is red with blue lettering and shows the sewn-on *Taag Yechida* the Southern Command. Her waist-belt and 9mm Browning holster are white and her lanyard red; she also wears the new-style IDF fatigue hat with IDF name-plate. (IDF Spokesman)

130. An Israeli reservist checks the papers of a Lebanese woman at an Awali River checkpoint in the winter of 1982. He is wearing the IDF kevlar flak jacket and one-piece winter coveralls, and carries an AK-47. (IMoD)

▲129 ▼130